Impressum
Verlag: BABADADA GmbH, Nedderfeld 112 , 22529 Hamburg
Geschäftsführer / Verlagsleitung: Harald Hof
Druck: Books on Demand GmbH, In de Tarpen 42, 22848 Norderstedt

Imprint
Publisher: BABADADA GmbH, Nedderfeld 112 , 22529 Hamburg, Germany
Managing Director / Publishing direction: Harald Hof
Print: Books on Demand GmbH, In de Tarpen 42, 22848 Norderstedt

classroom
教室

divide
除

186/2

board
黑板

school yard
校園

teacher
老師

paper
紙

write
書寫

pen
筆

desk
辦公桌

ruler
直尺

book
書

pupil
學生

satchel
書包

pencil case
鉛筆盒

pencil
鉛筆

pencil sharpener
削鉛筆機

rubber
橡皮擦

drawing pad
畫板

drawing
圖畫

paintbrush
畫筆

paint box
顏料盒

scissors
剪刀

glue
膠水

exercise book
練習冊

homework
家庭作業

12

number
數字

2+2

add
加

5-2

subtract
減

2×2

multiply
乘

calculate
計算

A

letter
字母

ABCDEFG
HIJKLMN
OPQRSTU
VWXYZ

alphabet
字母表

hello

word
字

text

課文

read

讀

chalk

粉筆

lesson

上課

register

登記

examination

考試

certificate

證書

school uniform

校服

education

教育

encyclopedia

百科全書

university

大學

microscope

顯微鏡

map

地圖

waste-paper basket

廢紙簍

hotel
飯店

hostel
青年旅社

currency exchange office
外幣兌換處

car
汽車

language
語言

yes / no
是/否

Okay
好的

hello
您好

translator
翻譯人員

Thank you
謝謝

how much is…?

……多少錢？

I don´t get it

我不明白

problem

問題

Good evening!

晚上好！

Good morning!

早上好！

Good night!

晚安！

goodbye

再見

direction

方向

luggage

行李

bag

包

backpack

背包

guest

客人

room

房間

sleeping bag

睡袋

tent

帳篷

tourist information

旅行資訊

beach

海灘

credit card

信用卡

breakfast

早餐

lunch

午餐

dinner

晚餐

Ticket

票

elevator

電梯

stamp

郵票

border

邊界

customs

海關

embassy

大使館

visa

簽證

passport

護照

airplane
飛機

ship
船

fire truck
消防車

truck
卡車

bus
公車

motorboat
汽艇

car
汽車

bike
腳踏車

ferry

渡輪

boat

小船

motorbike

機車

police car

警車

racing car

賽車

rental car

租車

car sharing

拼車

tow truck

拖車

garbage truck

垃圾車

engine

馬達

fuel

汽油

fuel station

加油站

traffic sign

交通標識

traffic

交通

traffic jam

交通堵塞

parking lot

停車場

train station

火車站

tracks

軌道

train

火車

tram

路面電車

wagon

客車廂

transport - 交通運送

helicopter

直升機

airport

機場

tower

塔

passenger

乘客

container

集裝箱

carton

紙板箱

cart

手推車

basket

籃子

take off / land

起飛/降落

city

城市

village

村莊

city center

市中心

house

房子

movie theater
電影院

advert
廣告

street light
路燈

street
街道

taxi
計程車

snack shop
小吃店

pedestrian
行人

sidewalk
人行道

zebra crossing
斑馬線

dumpster
垃圾箱

crossing
十字路口

traffic lights
紅綠燈

CINEMA

hut

小屋

apartment

公寓

train station

火車站

city hall

市政廳

museum

博物館

MUSEUM

school

學校

university

大學

bank

銀行

hospital

醫院

hotel

飯店

pharmacy

藥房

office

辦公室

book shop

書店

shop

商店

flower shop

花店

supermarket

超市

market

市場

department store

百貨商店

fishmonger's shop

魚店

mall

購物中心

harbor

海港

city - 城市

park

公園

bench

長凳

bridge

橋

stairs

樓梯

subway

捷運

tunnel

隧道

bus stop

公車站

bar

酒吧

restaurant

餐館

postbox

郵筒

street sign

路標

parking meter

停車計時器

zoo

動物園

swimming pool

游泳池

mosque

清真寺

farm
農場

pollution
污染

cemetery
墓地

church
教堂

playground
操場

temple
寺廟

landscape
地形

signpost
指示牌

path
路

meadow
草地

stone
石頭

hiker
徒步旅行
者

tree
樹

river
河

grass
草

flower
花

valley

峽谷

hill

丘陵

lake

湖

forest

森林

desert

沙漠

volcano

火山

castle

城堡

rainbow

彩虹

mushroom

蘑菇

palm tree

棕櫚樹

mosquito

蚊子

fly

蒼蠅

ant

螞蟻

bee

蜜蜂

spider

蜘蛛

beetle

甲蟲

frog

青蛙

squirrel

松鼠

hedgehog

刺蝟

hare

野兔

owl

貓頭鷹

bird

鳥

swan

天鵝

boar

野豬

deer

鹿

moose

麋鹿

dam

水壩

wind turbine

風力發電機

solar panel

太陽能電池板

climate

氣候

waiter
服務生

menu
菜譜

chair
椅子

soup
湯

pizza
披薩餅

cutlery
餐具

tablecloth
桌布

starter
前菜

main course
主菜

dessert
甜點

drinks
飲料

food
食物

bottle
瓶子

fast food

速食

street food

街邊小吃

teapot

茶壺

sugar bowl

糖盒

portion

一份飯菜

espresso machine

義式咖啡機

high chair

高腳椅

bill

帳單

tray

托盤

knife

刀

fork

餐叉

spoon

勺子

teaspoon

茶匙

serviette

餐巾

glass

玻璃杯

plate

碟子

soup plate

湯盤

saucer

碟子

sauce

醬

salt shaker

鹽瓶

pepper mill

胡椒研磨罐

vinegar

醋

oil

食用油

spices

調味料

ketchup

番茄醬

mustard

芥末

mayonnaise

美乃滋

special offer
特價

customer
顧客

dairy products
乳製品

FOR

fruit
水果

shopping cart
購物車

butcher's shop

肉鋪

bakery

麵包店

weigh

稱重

vegetables

蔬菜

meat

肉

frozen food

冷凍食品

cold cuts

冷盤

canned food

罐頭食品

detergent

洗衣粉

candy

甜食

household products

日用品

cleaning products

清潔用品

sales representative

銷售員

cash register

收銀機

cashier

收銀員

shopping list

購物清單

opening hours

開放時間

wallet

錢包

credit card

信用卡

bag

袋子

plastic bag

塑膠袋

water

水

juice

果汁

milk

牛奶

coke

可樂

wine

紅酒

beer

啤酒

alcohol

酒

cocoa

可可

tea

茶

coffee

咖啡

espresso

義式濃縮咖啡

cappuccino

卡布奇諾

banana

香蕉

apple

蘋果

orange

柳丁

melon

西瓜

lemon

檸檬

carrot

胡蘿蔔

garlic

大蒜

bamboo

竹子

onion

洋蔥

mushroom

蘑菇

nuts

堅果

noodles

麵條

spaghetti

義大利麵

rice

米飯

salad

沙拉

fries

薯條

fried potatoes

炸馬鈴薯

pizza

披薩餅

hamburger

漢堡

sandwich

三明治

escalope

炸豬排

ham

火腿

salami

義大利臘腸

sausage

香腸

chicken

雞肉

roast

烤肉

fish

魚

porridge oats

燕麥片

muesli

木斯里

cornflakes

玉米片

flour

麵粉

croissant

牛角麵包

bread roll

麵包捲

bread

麵包

toast

吐司

cookies

餅乾

butter

奶油

curd

凝乳

cake

蛋糕

egg

蛋

fried egg

煎蛋

cheese

起司

ice cream

冰淇淋

sugar

糖

honey

蜂蜜

jelly

果醬

nougat cream

巧克力醬

curry

咖哩

goat

山羊

cow

奶牛

calf

小牛

pig

豬

piglet

小豬

bull

公牛

goose

鵝

duck

鴨

chick

小雞

hen

母雞

cockerel

公雞

rat

鼠

cat

貓

mouse

老鼠

ox

牛

dog

狗

dog house

狗屋

garden hose

花園澆水軟管

watering can

澆水壺

scythe

長柄大鐮刀

plow

犁

sickle

鐮刀

hoe

鋤頭

pitchfork

長柄草耙

axe

斧頭

pushcart

獨輪手推車

trough

飼料槽

milk can

牛奶罐

sack

麻布袋

fence

柵欄

stable

馬廄

greenhouse

溫室

soil

土壤

seed

種子

fertilizer

肥料

combine harvester

聯合收割機

harvest

收割

harvest

收割

yams

地瓜

wheat

小麥

soya

大豆

potato

土豆

corn

玉米

rapeseed

油菜籽

fruit tree

果樹

manioc

樹薯

grain

穀物

living room
....
客廳

bathroom
....
浴室

kitchen
....
廚房

bedroom
....
臥室

kids room
....
兒童房

dining room
....
餐廳

floor

地板

wall

牆壁

ceiling

天花板

cellar

地窖

sauna

三溫暖

balcony

陽臺

terrace

露臺

pool

游泳池

lawn mower

割草機

sheet

被單

bedspread

床罩

bed

床

broom

掃帚

bucket

水桶

switch

開關

carpet

地毯

drape

窗簾

table

餐桌

chair

椅子

rocking chair

搖椅

armchair

扶手椅

book

書

blanket

毯子

decoration

裝飾品

firewood

木柴

film

電影

stereo system

高傳真音響

key

鑰匙

newspaper

報紙

painting

油畫

poster

海報

radio

收音機

notebook

筆記本

vacuum cleaner

吸塵器

cactus

仙人掌

candle

蠟燭

fridge
冰箱

microwave oven
微波爐

kitchen scales
廚房秤

toaster
烤麵包機

laundry detergent
洗潔精

freezer
冰櫃

stove
烤箱

dishwasher
洗碗機

cooker

炊具

pot

鍋

cast-iron pot

鑄鐵鍋

wok / kadai

炒鍋

pan

平底鍋

kettle

水壺

steamer

蒸鍋

baking tray

烤盤

crockery

陶瓷鍋

mug

馬克杯

bowl

碗

chopsticks

筷子

ladle

長柄勺

spatula

鏟子

whisk

攪拌器

strainer

濾網

sieve

篩子

grater

磨碎機

mortar

研缽

barbecue

燒烤

fireplace

明火

chopping board
菜板

rolling pin
擀麵杖

corkscrew
開瓶器

can
罐子

can opener
開罐器

oven cloth
隔熱手套

sink
水槽

brush
刷子

sponge
海綿

blender
攪拌機

deep freezer
冷藏箱

baby bottle
奶瓶

tap
水龍頭

heating
供暖裝置

towel
毛巾

shower
淋浴

shower curtain
浴簾

bubble bath
泡沫浴

bathtub
浴缸

washing machine
洗衣機

glass
玻璃杯

tiles
瓷磚

tap
水龍頭

potty
便壺

sink
水槽

toilet
廁所

squat toilet
蹲便器

bidet
坐浴器

urinal
小便斗

toilet paper
廁紙

toilet brush
馬桶刷

toothbrush

牙刷

toothpaste

牙膏

dental floss

牙線

wash

洗

hand shower

手持式蓮蓬頭

douche

沖洗器

basin

洗臉盆

back brush

洗背刷

soap

肥皂

shower gel

沐浴露

shampoo

洗髮乳

flannel

法蘭絨

drain

排水

creme

乳霜

deodorant

除臭劑

mirror

鏡子

hand mirror

手鏡

razor

刮鬍刀

shaving foam

刮鬍泡沫

aftershave

鬚後水

comb

梳子

brush

刷子

hair-dryer

吹風機

hairspray

噴髮定型劑

makeup

化妝品

lipstick

唇膏

nail varnish

指甲油

cotton wool

化妝棉

nail scissors

指甲剪

perfume

香水

washbag

洗漱包

stool

凳子

weighing scales

計重秤

bathrobe

浴袍

rubber gloves

橡膠手套

tampon

衛生棉條

sanitary towel

衛生棉

chemical toilet

化學廁所

bathroom - 浴室

alarm clock
鬧鐘

cuddly toy
毛絨玩具

toy car
玩具車

rattle
撥浪鼓

doll's house
玩具屋

present
禮物

balloon

氣球

bed

床

stroller

嬰兒車

deck of cards

撲克牌

jigsaw

拼圖

comic

漫畫

lego bricks

樂高積木

toy blocks

積木玩具

action figure

公仔

romper suit

嬰兒服

frisbee

飛盤

mobile

床鈴玩具

board game

棋盤遊戲

dice

骰子

model train set

火車模型

pacifier

安撫奶嘴

party

派對

picture book

繪本

ball

球

doll

洋娃娃

play

玩

sandpit
沙坑

swing
鞦韆

toys
玩具

video game console
電玩遊戲

tricycle
三輪車

teddy bear
泰迪熊

wardrobe
衣櫃

clothing
衣服

socks
襪子

stockings
長襪

tights
緊身褲

scarf
圍巾

umbrella
雨傘

t-shirt
T恤

belt
皮帶

boots
靴子

slippers
拖鞋

sneakers
運動鞋

sandals	shoes	rubber boots
涼鞋	鞋	雨靴

underwear	bra	undershirt
內褲	胸罩	背心

body

身體

pants

褲子

jeans

牛仔褲

skirt

短裙

blouse

女式襯衫

shirt

襯衫

pullover

套頭衫

sweater

連帽上衣

blazer

西裝夾克

jacket

夾克

coat

外套

raincoat

雨衣

costume

套裝

dress

連衣裙

wedding dress

婚紗

suit
西裝

nightgown
睡袍

pajamas
睡衣

sari
莎麗

headscarf
頭巾

turban
包頭巾

burka
波卡

kaftan
卡夫坦

abaya
(阿拉伯式)長袍

swimsuit
泳衣

trunks
男式泳褲

shorts
短褲

tracksuit
運動服

apron
圍裙

gloves
手套

button

鈕扣

glasses

眼鏡

bracelet

手鏈

necklace

項鍊

ring

戒指

earring

耳環

cap

便帽

coat hanger

衣架

hat

帽子

tie

領帶

zip

拉鍊

helmet

安全帽

braces

背帶

school uniform

校服

uniform

制服

bib
圍兜

pacifier
安撫奶嘴

diaper
尿布

server
伺服器

filing cabinet
檔案櫃

printer
印表機

paper
紙

monitor
螢幕

mouse
滑鼠

desk
辦公桌

folder
資料夾

keyboard
鍵盤

chair
椅子

waste-paper basket
廢紙簍

computer
電腦

coffee mug
咖啡杯

calculator
計算機

internet
網際網路

laptop

筆記型電腦

letter

信件

message

簡訊

cell phone

行動電話

network

網路

photocopier

影印機

software

軟體

telephone

電話

plug socket

插座

fax machine

傳真機

form

表格

document

檔案

buy

買

pay

付錢

trade

交易

money

現金

dollar

美元

euro

歐元

yen

日元

rouble

盧布

Swiss franc

瑞士法郎

renminbi yuan

人民幣

rupee

盧比

cash point

提款處

currency exchange office

外幣兌換處

gold

金

silver

銀

oil

石油

energy

能源

price

價格

contract

合約

tax

稅金

stock

股票

work

工作

employee

職員

employer

老闆

factory

工廠

shop

商店

police officer
警官

fireman
消防員

pilot
飛行員

cook
廚師

doctor
醫師

gardener

園丁

carpenter

木匠

seamstress

裁縫

judge

法官

chemist

化學家

actor

演員

bus driver

公車司機

taxi driver

計程車司機

fisherman

漁夫

cleaning lady

清洗女工

roofer

屋頂工

waiter

服務生

hunter

獵人

painter

畫家

baker

麵包師

electrician

電工

builder

建築工人

engineer

工程師

butcher

屠夫

plumber

水管工

postman

郵差

soldier

士兵

architect

建築師

cashier

收銀員

florist

花農

hairdresser

理髮師

conductor

售票員

mechanic

機械技師

captain

船長

dentist

牙醫

scientist

科學家

rabbi

拉比

imam

伊瑪目

monk

和尚

pastor

牧師

hammer
鐵錘

pliers
鉗子

screwdriver
螺絲起子

wrench
扳手

torch
手電筒

excavator

挖掘機

toolbox

工具箱

ladder

梯子

saw

鋸子

nails

釘子

drill

鑽機

repair
修

shovel
鏟子

Damn!
糟糕！

dustpan
畚箕

paint can
油漆桶

screws
螺絲

musical instruments
樂器

drum set
打擊樂器

loud speaker
揚聲器

guitar
吉他

double bass
低音提琴

trumpet
小號

piano

鋼琴

violin

小提琴

bass

貝斯

timpani

定音鼓

drums

鼓

keyboard

電子琴

saxophone

薩克斯風

flute

長笛

microphone

麥克風

entrance
入口

tiger
老虎

cage
籠子

zebra
斑馬

animal feed
動物飼料

panda
熊貓

animals

動物

elephant

大象

kangaroo

袋鼠

rhino

犀牛

gorilla

大猩猩

bear

熊

camel

駱駝

ostrich

鴕鳥

lion

獅子

monkey

猴子

flamingo

紅鶴

parrot

鸚鵡

polar bear

北極熊

penguin

企鵝

shark

鯊魚

peacock

孔雀

snake

蛇

crocodile

鱷魚

zookeeper

動物園管理員

seal

海豹

jaguar

美洲豹

pony

矮種馬

leopard

豹

hippo

河馬

giraffe

長頸鹿

eagle

老鷹

boar

野豬

fish

魚

turtle

龜

walrus

海象

fox

狐狸

gazelle

羚羊

zoo - 動物園

American football
橄欖球

cycling
騎腳踏車

tennis
網球

basketball
籃球

swimming
游泳

boxing
拳擊

ice hockey
冰球

soccer
美式足球

badminton
羽毛球

athletics
田徑

handball
手球

skiing
滑雪

polo
馬球

write	draw	show
書寫	畫	展示

push	give	take
推	給	拿

have

有

do

做

be

當

stand

站

run

跑

pull

拉

throw

丟

fall

摔倒

lie

躺

wait

等待

carry

攜帶

sit

坐

get dressed

穿衣

sleep

睡覺

wake up

醒來

look at
看

cry
哭

stroke
擊

comb
梳頭

talk
交談

understand
明白

ask
問

listen
聽

drink
喝

eat
吃

tidy up
清理

love
愛

cook
做飯

drive
開車

fly
飛

sail

航行

calculate

計算

read

讀

learn

學習

work

工作

marry

結婚

sew

縫

brush teeth

刷牙

kill

殺

smoke

抽菸

send

寄

grandmother
祖母

grandfather
祖父

father
父親

mother
母親

baby
嬰兒

daughter
女兒

son
兒子

guest

客人

aunt

阿姨

uncle

叔叔

brother

兄弟

sister

姐妹

body

身體

forehead
前額

eye
眼睛

shoulder
肩膀

finger
手指

face
臉

chin
下巴

hand
手

breast
乳房

leg
腿

arm
手臂

baby

嬰兒

man

男人

woman

女人

girl

女孩

boy

男孩

head

頭

back
背部

belly
肚子

navel
肚臍

toe
腳趾

heel
腳後跟

bone
骨頭

hip
臀部

knee
膝蓋

elbow
手肘

nose
鼻子

buttocks
屁股

skin
皮膚

cheek
臉頰

ear
耳朵

lip
嘴唇

body - 身體

mouth

嘴

tooth

牙齒

tongue

舌頭

brain

腦

heart

心臟

muscle

肌肉

lung

肺

liver

肝臟

stomach

胃

kidneys

腎臟

sex

性交

condom

保險套

ovum

卵子

semen

精子

pregnancy

懷孕

menstruation

月事

vagina

陰道

penis

陰莖

eyebrow

眉毛

hair

頭髮

neck

脖子

hospital
醫院

ambulance
急救車

wheelchair
輪椅

fracture
骨折

doctor

醫師

emergency room

急診室

nurse

護理師

emergency

緊急情形

unconscious

昏迷

pain

痛

injury

受傷

bleeding

出血

heart attack

心臟病發作

stroke

中風

allergy

過敏

cough

咳嗽

fever

發燒

flu

流感

diarrhea

腹瀉

headache

頭痛

cancer

癌症

diabetes

糖尿病

surgeon

外科醫師

scalpel

手術刀

operation

手術

CT

電腦斷層掃描

x-ray

X光

ultrasound

超音波

face mask

口罩

disease

疾病

waiting room

候診室

crutch

拐杖

plaster

石膏

bandage

繃帶

injection

注射

stethoscope

聽診器

stretcher

擔架

clinical thermometer

體溫計

birth

出生

overweight

超重

hearing aid

助聽器

disinfectant

消毒液

infection

感染

virus

病毒

HIV / AIDS

愛滋病

medicine

藥物

vaccination

接種疫苗

tablets

藥片

pill

藥丸

emergency call

急救電話

blood pressure monitor

血壓計

ill / healthy

生病/健康

Help!
救命！

alarm
警報

assault
突擊

attack
攻擊

danger
危險

emergency exit
緊急出口

Fire!
失火了！

fire extinguisher
滅火器

accident
意外

first-aid kit
急救箱

SOS
呼救訊號

police
員警

Europe

歐洲

North America

北美洲

South America

南美洲

Africa

非洲

Asia

亞洲

Australia

澳洲

Atlantic

大西洋

Pacific

太平洋

Indian Ocean

印度洋

Antarctic Ocean

南冰洋

Arctic Ocean

北冰洋

North pole

北極

South pole
南極

Antarctica
南極洲

earth
地球

land
陸地

sea
海

island
島

nation
國家

state
州

clock face

錶盤

hour hand

時針

minute hand

分針

second hand

秒針

What time is it?

現在幾點？

day

天

time

時間

now

現在

digital watch

電子錶

minute

分

hour

時

week
週

Monday 週一 **MO**

Tuesday 週二

Wednesday 週三 **W**

TU

TH

Thursday 週四

Saturday 週六

Friday 週五 **FR**

SA

SO

Sunday 週日

yesterday

昨天

today

今天

tomorrow

明天

morning

早晨

noon

中午

evening

晚上

workdays

工作日

weekend

週末

rain
雨

spring
春

summer
夏

wind
風

fall
秋

snow
雪

winter
冬

weather forecast

天氣預告

thermometer

溫度計

sunshine

陽光

cloud

雲

fog

霧

humidity

潮濕

lightning

閃電

thunder

打雷

storm

風暴

hail

冰雹

monsoon

季風

flood

洪水

ice

冰

January

一月

February

二月

March

三月

April

四月

May

五月

June

六月

July

七月

August

八月

September

九月

October

十月

November

十一月

December

十二月

shapes
形狀

circle

圓形

square

正方形

rectangle

長方形

triangle

三角形

sphere

球體

cube

立方體

colors
顏色

white

白

yellow

黃

orange

橙

pink

粉

red

紅

purple

紫

blue

藍

green

綠

brown

棕

gray

灰

black

黑

a lot / a little

很多/少許

angry / calm

生氣/平靜

beautiful / ugly

美/醜

beginning / end

首/尾

big / small

大/小

bright / dark

明/暗

brother / sister

兄弟/姐妹

clean / dirty

乾淨/骯髒

complete / incomplete

完整/缺失

day / night

白天/晚上

dead / alive

死/生

wide / narrow

寬/窄

edible / inedible

可食用/非食用

evil / kind

邪惡/善良

excited / bored

興奮/無聊

fat / thin

胖/瘦

first / last

第一/最後

friend / enemy

朋友/敵人

full / empty

滿/空

hard / soft

硬/軟

heavy / light

重/輕

hunger / thirst

餓/渴

ill / healthy

生病/健康

illegal / legal

非法/合法

intelligent / stupid

聰明/愚笨

left / right

左/右

near / far

近/遠

new / used

新/舊

nothing / something

沒有/有些

old / young

老/幼

on / off

開/關

open / closed

打開/闔上

quiet / loud

安靜/吵鬧

rich / poor

富/窮

right / wrong

對/錯

rough / smooth

粗糙/光滑

sad / happy

傷心/高興

short / long

短/長

slow / fast

慢/快

wet / dry

濕/乾

warm / cool

溫暖/涼爽

war / peace

戰爭/和平

數字

0

zero

零

1

one

一

2

two

二

3

three

三

4

four

四

5

five

五

6

six

六

7

seven

七

8

eight

八

9

nine

九

10

ten

十

11

eleven

十一

12

twelve

十二

13

thirteen

十三

14

fourteen

十四

15

fifteen

十五

16

sixteen

十六

17

seventeen

十七

18

eighteen

十八

19

nineteen

十九

20

twenty

二十

100

hundred

百

1.000

thousand

千

1.000.000

million

百萬

languages
語言

English

英語

American English

美式英語

Chinese Mandarin

普通話

Hindi

印地語

Spanish

西班牙語

French

法語

Arabic

阿拉伯語

Russian

俄語

Portuguese

葡萄牙語

Bengali

孟加拉語

German

德語

Japanese

日語

I

我

you

你

he / she / it

他/她/它

we

我們

you

你們

they

他們

who?

誰？

what?

什麼？

how?

如何？

where?

何處？

when?

何時？

name

名字

behind

後面

in

裡面

in front of

前面

over

上方

on

上面

under

下麵

beside

旁邊

between

中間

place

地點